# bruschetta

crostini and other Italian snacks

MAXINE CLARK

# bruschetta
crostini and other Italian snacks

PHOTOGRAPHY BY GUS FILGATE

RYLAND
PETERS
& SMALL
LONDON NEW YORK

First published in Great Britain in 2003
by Ryland Peters & Small
Kirkman House
12–14 Whitfield Street,
London W1T 2RP
www.rylandpeters.com

10 9 8 7 6 5 4 3 2 1

**ISBN 1 84172 399 1**

A catalogue record for this book is available from
the British Library.

**Printed in China**

**Designer**  Catherine Griffin
**Commissioning Editor**  Elsa Petersen-Schepelern
**Editor**  Sharon Ashman
**Production**  Tamsin Curwood
**Art Director**  Gabriella Le Grazie
**Publishing Director**  Alison Starling

**Food Stylist**  Maxine Clark
**Assistant Food Stylist**  Becca Hetherston
**Props Stylist**  Helen Trent

**Notes**

All spoon measurements are level
unless otherwise indicated.

All eggs are medium, unless otherwise
specified. Uncooked or partly cooked
eggs should not be served to the very
young, the very old, the frail, or to
pregnant women.

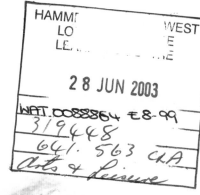

319448

# contents

# toast with taste ...

I first experienced bruschetta in an Italian friend's farmhouse in the beautiful Tuscan hills. We had just been out to collect sweet chestnuts and had done quite a bit of climbing to get to the trees. We were starving and it wasn't yet time for supper. So on our return, my friend decided to make us all *fettunta* – the Tuscan word for bruschetta rubbed with raw garlic and smeared with a ripe tomato. He toasted some huge, thick slices of Tuscan unsalted bread over some glowing embers on the hearth, cut a large juicy clove of garlic in half and rubbed it over the toasted bread, then drizzled it with a local green, peppery olive oil. Finally, he spread a few roughly crushed tomatoes over the top. We devoured these bruschetta in our hands in front of the restoked fire – one of the best snacks I have ever eaten. And that is just what bruschetta are – satisfying snacks with peasant origins.

Crostini, on the other hand, are smaller, more refined snacks, usually baked in the oven or fried until crisp. These are elegantly served with pre-dinner drinks and are frequently offered as a matter of course in Italian bars. Crostoni, just larger crostini, are nice and crunchy, and vehicles for any combination of ingredients. In the northern regions of Italy, particularly the Veneto, crostini are made using fried or grilled polenta as the base. A very filling mouthful indeed, they have an interesting contrast of textures – crisp on the outside, soft inside.

Whatever their size or shape, all these snacks should be freshly made with the best ingredients. Bruschetta and crostini have sneaked their way into our modern lifestyles, appearing at smart dinner parties as starters and at cocktail parties as pre-dinner nibbles – far removed from their humble peasant origins, but none the worse for that. After all, we all love toast and to be truthful, that's what they are!

# the basics

True bruschetta (and it is pronounced 'brooskayta' not 'brooshetta') is a large slice of country bread toasted on the barbecue or over a wood fire and then rubbed with garlic, sometimes topped with a crushed tomato and anointed with olive oil. It is a popular snack found all over Italy, served in bars and at home. A true crostoni (large) or crostini (small) is brushed with olive oil and cooked in the oven or under the grill, or fried in olive oil or butter.

## bruschetta

4 thick slices country bread, preferably sourdough

2 garlic cloves, halved

extra virgin olive oil, for drizzling

**Serves 4**

Grill, toast or pan-grill the bread on both sides until lightly charred or toasted. Rub the top side of each slice with the cut garlic and drizzle with olive oil. Keep warm in a low oven before adding your chosen topping.

## crostini

1 Italian sfilatino* or thin French baguette

extra virgin olive oil, for brushing

**Serves 6**

* A sfilatino is a long, thin loaf available from Italian delicatessens and larger supermarkets.

Preheat the oven to 190°C (375°F) Gas 5. Slice the bread into thin rounds, brush both sides of each slice with olive oil and spread out on a baking sheet. Bake for about 10 minutes until crisp and golden. Let cool, then keep in an airtight container until ready to use. It is best to reheat them in the oven before adding the topping.

Crostoni are simply cut from a larger loaf and prepared in the same way as crostini.

## polenta crostini

300 g polenta flour

extra virgin olive oil, for brushing, or butter, for frying

**Serves 6–8**

Make the polenta by slowly sprinkling the flour into 1 litre of salted, boiling water. Cook over a low heat for 45 minutes, stirring occasionally. Turn out into a mound onto a wooden board. Let cool and set. Alternatively, use the quick-cook version (cook according to the manufacturer's instructions), or even the ready-made kind sold in a block. Slice the cooled and set polenta into the thickness you want, and cut or stamp out the required shape and size. Melt a little butter in a hot, non-stick frying pan and cook until crisp, turning once. Alternatively, brush both sides with olive oil or melted butter and cook on a stove-top grill pan, turning once, if you prefer a char-grilled taste.

**vegetables**

A wonderful combination of fresh spring flavours and colours. Puréeing the peas gives a sweet, earthy base on which to sprinkle the combination of salty, nutty Pecorino (Parmesan would work very well here, too) and fruity pears tossed in a few drops of balsamic vinegar for sharpness. A delicious start to a light dinner party.

# **pear, pecorino and pea** crostini

1 Italian sfilatino or thin French baguette, sliced into thin rounds

extra virgin olive oil, for brushing and moistening

250 g shelled fresh or frozen peas

freshly grated nutmeg

1 small ripe pear

a drop balsamic or sherry vinegar

125 g fresh young Pecorino or Parmesan cheese, diced

sea salt and freshly ground black pepper

**Serves 6**

Preheat the oven to 190°C (375°F) Gas 5. To make the crostini, brush both sides of each slice of bread with olive oil and spread out on a baking sheet. Bake for about 10 minutes until crisp and golden.

Meanwhile, blanch the peas in boiling water for 3 minutes if they are fresh or 2 minutes if they are frozen. Drain them, refresh in cold water and drain again. Purée the peas in a food processor or blender, moistening with a little olive oil. Season with salt, pepper and freshly grated nutmeg. Core and finely chop the pear. Mix with a drop of balsamic or sherry vinegar, then add the cheese and mix well. Spread the crostini with a mound of pea purée and top with a spoonful of the pear and cheese mixture. Serve immediately.

# slow-roasted tomatoes on bruschetta with salted ricotta or feta

These firm but juicy roasted tomatoes burst with the flavour of the sun. They take no time to prepare but a long time concentrating their flavours in the oven – they smell fantastic while cooking! Plum tomatoes have less moisture in them and work well. You can use other vine-ripened varieties – just make sure they have some taste!

Preheat the oven to 170°C (325°F) Gas 3. If using plum tomatoes cut them in half lengthways, if using round ones cut them in half crossways. Put them cut side up on a baking sheet. Mix the garlic and oregano with the olive oil, salt and pepper. Spoon or brush this mixture over the cut tomatoes. Bake for about 2 hours, checking them occasionally. They should be slightly shrunk and still a brilliant red colour. If they are too dark they will be bitter. Let cool.

To make the bruschetta, grill, toast or pan-grill the bread on both sides until lightly charred or toasted. Cut the bruschetta slices to size so that 2 tomato halves will sit on top of each one. Rub the top side of each slice with the cut garlic, then drizzle with olive oil.

Put 2 tomato halves on each bruschetta, sprinkle with the slivered cheese and top with a basil leaf, if liked. Serve at room temperature.

8 large ripe plum tomatoes

2 garlic cloves, finely chopped

1 tablespoon dried oregano

4 tablespoons extra virgin olive oil

50 g salted ricotta or feta cheese, thinly sliced

sea salt and freshly ground black pepper

basil leaves, to serve (optional)

### for the bruschetta:

4 thick slices country bread, preferably sourdough

2 garlic cloves, halved

extra virgin olive oil, for drizzling

**Serves 4**

# egg, mascarpone and asparagus crostini

This is a creamy light topping, packed with the flavour of asparagus. For the best results, don't be tempted to make this with anything other than fresh asparagus. If you have some, you can drizzle a little truffle oil over for a special occasion, as the flavours of eggs and truffle go very well together.

Preheat the oven to 190°C (375°F) Gas 5. To make the crostini, brush both sides of each slice of bread with olive oil and spread out on a baking sheet. Bake for about 10 minutes until crisp and golden.

Meanwhile, beat the butter with the parsley and spring onions and season with salt and pepper.

Cook the asparagus in boiling salted water for about 6 minutes until tender. Cut off and reserve the tips and slice the stems.

Boil the eggs for 6-8 minutes. Plunge into cold water for a couple of minutes, then shell and roughly mash with a fork. Add the spring onion mixture and mascarpone and stir until creamy. Fold in the sliced asparagus stems, then season with salt and pepper.

Spread the egg mixture thickly onto the crostini, top with the asparagus tips and drizzle with a couple of drops of truffle oil, if using, or some extra virgin olive oil. Serve immediately.

1 Italian sfilatino or thin French baguette, sliced into thin rounds

extra virgin olive oil, for brushing

125 g unsalted butter, softened

4 tablespoons chopped fresh parsley

4 spring onions, finely chopped

12 spears fresh green asparagus, stems trimmed

6 large eggs

4–6 tablespoons mascarpone cheese, softened

truffle oil, for drizzling (optional)

sea salt and freshly ground black pepper

**Serves 6**

# cherry tomato, bocconcini and basil bruschetta

All the colours of the Italian flag are here – red, white and green. This makes a great start to a rustic summer meal. Bocconcini (meaning 'little bites') are tiny balls of mozzarella. They are the perfect size for bruschetta but, if you can't find them, use regular mozzarella instead and cut it into cubes.

Whisk 3 tablespoons of the olive oil with the balsamic vinegar. Season to taste with salt and pepper. Stir in the halved bocconcini or mozarella cubes, tomatoes and torn basil leaves.

To make the bruschetta, grill, toast or pan-grill the bread on both sides until lightly charred or toasted. Rub the top side of each slice with the cut garlic, then drizzle with olive oil.

Cover each slice of bruschetta with rocket and spoon over the tomatoes and mozzarella. Drizzle with the remaining olive oil and top with fresh basil leaves.

4 tablespoons extra virgin olive oil

1 teaspoon balsamic vinegar

12 bocconcini cheeses, halved, or 375 g regular mozzarella cheese, cubed

20 ripe cherry tomatoes or pomodorini (baby plum tomatoes), halved

a handful of torn fresh basil leaves, plus extra to serve

125 g rocket

sea salt and freshly ground black pepper.

for the bruschetta:

4 thick slices country bread, preferably sourdough

2 garlic cloves, halved

extra virgin olive oil, for drizzling

**Serves 4**

# **white bean and black olive** crostini

The combination of bland creamy beans and sharp, rich, salty tapenade makes a sublime mouthful, especially when spread on crisp crostini. You can use any type of canned bean for this, but the whiter they are the prettier they look. If you like, chop up some more black olives and sprinkle them on the bean purée or crumble some crisply cooked bacon over the top for extra crunch.

To make the tapenade, put the olives, garlic, anchovies, capers and olive oil into a blender or food processor and blend until smooth. Scrape out into a jar, cover with a layer of olive oil and set aside.

Preheat the oven to 190°C (375°F) Gas 5. To make the crostini, brush both sides of each slice of bread with olive oil and spread out on a baking sheet. Bake for about 10 minutes until crisp and golden.

Meanwhile, make the bean purée. Heat the oil in a small frying pan and add the garlic. Cook gently for 2 minutes until golden but don't let it turn brown. Stir in the rosemary and chilli. Remove from the heat, add the beans and 3 tablespoons of water. Mash the beans roughly with a fork and return to the heat until warmed through. Taste and season with salt and pepper.

Spread a layer of tapenade on the crostini followed by a spoonful of bean purée. Scatter with the chopped parsley and serve immediately.

**for the tapenade:**

175 g Greek-style black olives, such as Kalamata, pitted

2 garlic cloves

3 canned anchovies, drained

2 teaspoons capers, drained

1 tablespoon olive oil

**for the crostini:**

1 Italian sfilatino or thin French baguette, sliced into thin rounds

extra virgin olive oil, for brushing

**for the white bean purée:**

2 tablespoons olive oil

2 garlic cloves, finely chopped

1 teaspoon very finely chopped fresh rosemary

1 small red chilli, deseeded and finely chopped

400 g canned cannellini beans, rinsed and drained

sea salt and freshly ground black pepper

**to serve:**

chopped fresh parsley

**Serves 6–8**

The word *fettunta* comes from the Tuscan dialect and derives from Latin, meaning 'anointed slice'. It is a slice of bread grilled over hot coals, rubbed with garlic and drizzled with olive oil. To be authentic you should use only the finest Tuscan extra virgin olive oil. The ripe tomato is just crushed in your hand and smashed onto the bread, then eaten immediately. This is bruschetta at its simplest and best. This is a more civilized version, but you should try the real thing – it's great fun! Use only the best and freshest ingredients for this.

# **traditional peasant tomato and garlic** bruschetta (*fettunta*)

Roughly chop the tomatoes and season with salt and pepper.

To make the bruschetta, grill, toast or pan-grill the bread on both sides until lightly charred or toasted. Rub the top side of each slice with the cut garlic, then drizzle with olive oil.

Spoon the tomatoes over the bruschetta and drizzle with more olive oil. Eat immediately with your fingers!

4 large very ripe tomatoes

4 thick slices country bread, preferably sourdough

2 garlic cloves, halved

extra virgin olive oil, for drizzling

sea salt and freshly ground black pepper

**Serves 4**

# olive oil and garlic bruschetta

This is pared-down simplicity and so easy to make. It beats the likes of doughballs and garlic bread hands down. The most important thing is not to overcook the garlic – it must on no account turn brown. This is great served instead of garlic bread with a selection of salads.

Slice the garlic lengthways into paper-thin slices. Heat a small pan, pour in the olive oil and stir in the garlic. Cook until the garlic starts to give off its aroma and is golden but not brown (or it will taste bitter). Remove from the heat, then mix in the chilli flakes and parsley, if using. Cover to keep warm.

To make the bruschetta, grill, toast or pan-grill the bread on both sides until lightly charred or toasted, then drizzle with olive oil. Spoon or brush over the garlicky chilli oil. Eat immediately with your fingers!

4 large garlic cloves

6 tablespoons extra virgin olive oil

a good pinch chilli flakes

4 tablespoons chopped fresh parsley (optional)

### for the bruschetta:

4 thick slices country bread, preferably sourdough

extra virgin olive oil, for drizzling

**Serves 4**

This is a joy to make when fresh artichokes are in season. After preparing the artichokes, they are halved and fried in butter until tender. The pesto and pine nuts are perfect foils for the slightly bitter taste of the artichoke. If fresh ones are not available, you can use frozen or canned artichokes, or those preserved in oil. Whichever you use, always lightly fry them to bring out their full flavour.

# **artichoke, pesto and pine nut** bruschetta

To make the bruschetta, grill, toast or pan-grill the bread on both sides until lightly charred or toasted. Rub the top side of each slice with the cut garlic, then drizzle with olive oil. Keep them warm in a low oven.

Prepare the artichokes (see note below) and cut them in half. Heat the oil and butter in a frying pan, add the artichokes and fry gently until they are completely tender and beginning to brown. Splash in the balsamic vinegar, turn up the heat and toss the artichokes until the vinegar evaporates.

To make the pesto Genovese, put the garlic, pine nuts, grated Parmesan, basil leaves, olive oil and seasoning in a blender or food processor and blend until smooth.

Spread the bruschetta with the pesto and divide the artichokes between the slices. Scatter with the pine nuts and Parmesan shavings. Serve immediately.

**Note:** To prepare fresh artichokes, first fill a bowl with water and squeeze in the juice of half a lemon. Use the other lemon half to rub the cut portions of the artichokes as you work. Trim the artichokes by snapping off the dark green outer leaves, starting at the base. Trim the stalk to about 5 cm and peel it. Cut about 1 cm off the tip of the artichoke, then place them in the lemony water until required.

4 thick slices country bread, preferably sourdough
2 garlic cloves, halved
extra virgin olive oil, for brushing

for the artichoke topping:
6 small, fresh artichokes, each about 8 cm long
2 tablespoons olive oil
25 g butter
1 tablespoon balsamic vinegar

for the pesto genovese:
2 garlic cloves
50 g pine nuts
4 tablespoons freshly grated Parmesan cheese
50 g fresh basil leaves
150 ml extra virgin olive oil
sea salt and freshly ground black pepper

to serve:
2 tablespoons pine nuts, toasted
shavings of Parmesan cheese

**Serves 4**

Preheat the oven to 240°C (475°F) Gas 9. Put the peppers into a large roasting tin and roast for 20-30 minutes, turning once, until they begin to char. Remove from the oven and put into a plastic bag, seal tightly and set aside for 10 minutes to steam off the skins.

Meanwhile, to make the bruschetta, grill or pan-grill the slices of bread on one side only until lightly charred or toasted. Rub the grilled sides with the cut garlic, then drizzle with olive oil. Keep them warm in a low oven.

Remove the peppers from the bag and peel off the skins, then pull out the stalks - the seeds should come with them. Cut the peppers in half, scrape out any remaining seeds and slice the flesh thickly.

To make the caper dressing, put the chopped capers into a bowl, then stir in the olive oil, vinegar, salt and pepper.

Spread the pesto over the ungrilled side of the bruschetta and put 2 slices of cheese on each one. Cook under a preheated grill for 1-2 minutes or until the cheese is beginning to melt and turn golden (watch that the bread doesn't catch and burn).

Remove from the heat and put a tangle of roasted peppers on top and drizzle with the caper dressing. Serve immediately.

2 sweet red peppers

4 tablespoons Pesto Genovese (see page 25)

8 thick slices goats' cheese with rind

**for the bruschetta:**

4 thick slices country bread, preferably sourdough

2 garlic cloves, halved

extra virgin olive oil, for drizzling

**for the caper dressing:**

2 tablespoons salted capers, soaked in water for 10 minutes, then rinsed and chopped

3 tablespoons extra virgin olive oil

1 teaspoon balsamic vinegar

sea salt and freshly ground black pepper

**Serves 4**

# goats' cheese and sweet red peppers on bruschetta

Cooked goats' cheese is a relative newcomer to Italian cuisine. When grilled, its sharp, creamy texture perfectly partners the smoky sweetness of roasted red peppers, especially when topped with salty, pungent capers and a little dressing.

# garlic mushrooms with gremolata on bruschetta

A grown-up version of mushrooms on toast. Don't be tempted to use button or shiitake mushrooms: the first are too bland, the second too strong. If you have the good fortune to have some wild mushrooms, try a combination of porcini and girolles or chanterelles. Make sure they don't become overcooked and soggy though. Top with a fried or poached egg for a substantial snack.

To make the bruschetta, preheat a stove-top grill pan, add the slices of bread and cook on both sides until barred with brown. Brush with melted butter and keep them warm in a low oven.

To make the gremolata, put the garlic, lemon zest, parsley and olives into a bowl, stir well, cover and chill.

Then, prepare the garlic mushrooms. Melt the butter or heat the olive oil in a frying pan, add the shallots and garlic and fry for 5 minutes until soft and golden. Add the mushrooms and toss well. Fry over high heat for 1 minute.

Add the wine and season with salt and pepper. Cook over high heat again until the wine evaporates. Stir in the parsley. Pile the mushrooms on the bruschetta and serve immediately, topped with a sprinkling of gremolata, if using.

4 thick slices country bread, preferably sourdough

melted butter, for brushing

**for the black olive gremolata (optional):**

1 small garlic clove, finely chopped

finely grated zest of 1 lemon

4 tablespoons chopped fresh flat leaf parsley

16 Greek-style black olives, such as kalamata, pitted and chopped

**for the garlic mushrooms:**

75 g butter or olive oil

3 shallots, finely chopped

2 garlic cloves, finely chopped

500 g large mushrooms, thickly sliced

5 tablespoons dry white wine

3 tablespoons chopped fresh flat leaf parsley

sea salt and freshly ground black pepper

**Serves 4**

Baba Ganoush is a Middle Eastern dip, usually served with a flatbread. It makes a perfect topping for crostini, and could almost be Sicilian with its mixture of aubergine and sesame seed flavours. Although sesame seed paste is unknown in Sicily, sesame seeds are commonly used in baking, especially to flavour breads.

# baba ganoush crostini topped with crispy aubergines

Preheat a stove-top grill pan until very hot. Prick the aubergine all over with a sharp knife, then pan-grill, turning regularly, until blackened and completely soft. This will take about 20 minutes. Let cool slightly, then remove the charred skin. Roughly chop the flesh, put it in a sieve and let drain. Press to remove the bitter juices.

Put the aubergine flesh in a blender or food processor with the tahini, crushed garlic and a pinch of hot paprika. Blend until well-mixed, then stir in the parsley or coriander. Taste, then season with lemon juice, salt and pepper.

To make the crispy aubergines, heat the oil in a frying pan and add the thinly sliced aubergine. Cook until brown and crisp. Remove with a slotted spoon and drain on kitchen paper.

Preheat the oven to 190°C (375°F) Gas 5. To make the crostini, brush both sides of each slice of bread with olive oil and spread out on a baking sheet. Bake for about 10 minutes until crisp and golden.

Put a slice of tomato on each crostini, season with salt, then spoon on a mound of baba ganoush and top with a slice of crispy aubergine. Drizzle with olive oil and sprinkle with hot paprika. Serve immediately.

1 aubergine, about 450 g

3 tablespoons tahini (sesame seed paste)

1 garlic clove, crushed

pinch hot paprika, plus extra for serving

2 tablespoons chopped fresh parsley or coriander

juice of 1 lemon

3 large ripe tomatoes, very thinly sliced

extra virgin olive oil, for drizzling

sea salt and freshly ground black pepper

for the crispy aubergines:

vegetable oil, for shallow frying

1 small aubergine, very thinly sliced

for the crostini:

1 Italian sfilatino or thin French baguette, sliced into thin rounds

extra virgin olive oil, for brushing

**Serves 6**

**fish**

The contrast of strong flavours and interesting textures in this recipe transports you instantly to the shores of the Mediterranean. Use a mixture of green and black olives if you prefer a sharper flavour. This mixture can be used as a stuffing for tomatoes, too.

# tuna, black olive, pine nut and caper
## crostini

Preheat the oven to 190°C (375°F) Gas 5. To make the crostini, brush both sides of each slice of bread with olive oil and spread out on a baking sheet. Bake for about 10 minutes until crisp and golden.

Put the olives, pine nuts, capers, garlic, parsley, tomatoes and lemon rind in a bowl and mix well. Add the tuna, break it up with a fork and mix it thoroughly with the other ingredients. Moisten with a little olive oil, taste and season with salt and pepper. Pile the mixture on top of the crostini. Serve immediately.

1 Italian sfilatino or thin French baguette, thinly sliced diagonally

extra virgin olive oil, for brushing and moistening

175 g oven-baked or Greek-style black olives, pitted and chopped

2 tablespoons pine nuts, chopped

1 tablespoon capers, rinsed and chopped

1 small garlic clove, finely chopped

1 tablespoon chopped fresh parsley

6 sun-dried tomatoes, soaked and chopped

1 tablespoon finely grated lemon rind

100 g canned tuna in oil, drained

sea salt and freshly ground black pepper

**Serves 6**

# chilli squid and fried aubergine on bruschetta

The marinade tenderizes the squid and adds a kick of chilli to its natural sweetness – the longer it is marinated, the more tender it will become. The aubergine can be fried in advance then warmed up in the oven, leaving only the squid to be fried before serving. The rocket not only adds colour, but a peppery sharpness to cut through the richness of the squid and aubergine. You can of course use frozen squid for this.

To make the marinade, put the chillies, garlic, lemon rind, lemon juice, sugar and olive oil into a blender or food processor and blend until smooth. Stir the squid into the marinade, cover and leave for 2 hours.

To make the bruschetta, grill, toast or pan-grill the bread on both sides until lightly charred or toasted. Rub the top side of each slice with the cut garlic, then drizzle with olive oil. Keep warm in a low oven.

Preheat the oil in a wok or deep-fat fryer to 190°C (375°F) or until a piece of stale bread turns golden in a few seconds when dropped in. Deep-fry the aubergine slices in batches until brown and crisp. Remove with a slotted spoon and drain on kitchen paper, then arrange in an even layer over the bruschetta. Keep warm in a low oven.

Heat a heavy frying pan until it is very hot and brush with oil. Remove the squid from the marinade and drain well, reserving the marinade. Sauté the squid for about 1 minute, tossing all the time until just caramelizing. Pour the marinade into the pan and boil rapidly for 30 seconds to reduce. Spoon the squid over the aubergine slices. Serve immediately with some rocket piled on top and lemon wedges, if using.

**Note:** To clean fresh squid, pull the head from the body. Remove the plastic quill from the inside of the squid tube, then rinse the tubes. Trim the tentacles from the head. Pop out the beak from the centre of the tentacles. Rinse, discarding the head and entrails.

400 g baby squid, cleaned and sliced (see note below)

vegetable oil, for deep-frying

1 small aubergine, very thinly sliced

sea salt and freshly ground black pepper

### for the marinade:

2 small red chillies, deseeded and chopped

2 garlic cloves

finely grated rind and juice of 1 lemon

1 tablespoon sugar

4 tablespoons olive oil

### for the bruschetta:

4 thick slices country bread, preferably sourdough

2 garlic cloves, halved

extra virgin olive oil, for drizzling

### to serve:

115 g rocket

lemon wedges (optional)

**Serves 4**

# spicy garlic prawns with tomatoes and chickpeas on bruschetta

This is a very popular combination of ingredients in southern Italy. Sweet prawns and tomatoes contrast with earthy chickpeas, pungent garlic and a hint of fiery chilli. Great food for warm summer evenings in the garden.

Heat the oil in a large frying pan and add the garlic, fry until just turning golden then add the chilli and wine. Turn up the heat and boil fast to reduce the wine to almost nothing. Add the tomatoes (if you are using canned tomatoes add some sugar to bring out their flavour) and cook for 1-2 minutes until they start to soften. Stir in the prawns and chickpeas and bring to the boil. Simmer for 2-3 minutes. Stir in the parsley, taste and season with salt and pepper. Set aside.

To make the bruschetta, grill, toast or pan-grill the bread on both sides until lightly charred or toasted. Rub the top side of each slice with the cut garlic, then drizzle with olive oil. Spoon over the prawn mixture and serve immediately.

2 tablespoons extra virgin olive oil

2 garlic cloves, finely chopped

1/2 teaspoon dried chilli flakes

100 ml dry white wine

250 g ripe tomatoes, peeled and chopped, or canned tomatoes, chopped

1/2 teaspoon sugar (optional)

200 g raw, shelled prawns

4 tablespoons canned chickpeas, rinsed and drained

2 tablespoons chopped fresh flat leaf parsley

sea salt and freshly ground black pepper

for the bruschetta:

4 thick slices country bread, preferably sourdough

2 garlic cloves, halved

extra virgin olive oil, for drizzling

**Serves 4**

Preheat the oven to 190°C (375°F) Gas 5. To make the crostini, brush both sides of each slice of bread with olive oil and spread out on a baking sheet. Bake for about 10 minutes until crisp and golden. Let cool, then keep in an airtight container until ready to use. It is best to reheat them in the oven before adding the topping.

Cut the sole fillets diagonally across the grain into thin strips. Toss the fingers in the seasoned flour and shake off the excess. Next, dip the sole fingers into the beaten egg in batches, turning them until well coated. Give them a bit of a shake, then toss them in the breadcrumbs until evenly coated. Put them on a tray, making sure they don't touch, cover them with plastic kitchen wrap and refrigerate.

To make the tartare sauce, beat the watercress into the mayonnaise then fold in the tarragon, parsley, capers and gherkins. Taste and season well with salt and pepper.

Preheat the vegetable oil in a wok or deep-fat fryer to 190°C (375°C) or until a piece of stale bread turns golden in a few seconds when dropped in. Fry a few sole sticks at a time until crisp and golden. Drain each batch well on kitchen paper, then sprinkle with salt. Keep them warm in a low oven with the door slightly ajar (they will go soggy if it is closed) while you cook the rest. Spread the crostini with a good dollop of tartare sauce, then top each one with 2 or 3 sole sticks. Serve with a few sprigs of watercress and some lemon wedges.

1 Italian sfilatino or thin French baguette, sliced into thin rounds

extra virgin olive oil, for brushing

250 g thick sole fillets, skinned

2 tablespoons seasoned flour

1 egg, beaten

50–100 g breadcrumbs, toasted

vegetable oil, for deep-frying

sea salt and freshly ground black pepper

### for the watercress tartare sauce:

50 g watercress leaves, blanched, squeezed dry and very finely chopped

300 ml mayonnaise

1 teaspoon finely chopped fresh tarragon

2 tablespoons chopped fresh parsley

1 tablespoon capers, rinsed and chopped

2 tablespoons chopped gherkins

### to serve:

watercress sprigs

lemon wedges

**Serves 6**

# sole sticks with watercress tartare crostini

Crunchy fingers of freshly cooked sole sit on top of a delicious creamy, but sharp, tartare sauce tinged green with watercress. The difference between homemade and bought tartare sauce is immense – so make your own for this recipe and you'll thank yourself in the end.

# smoked salmon and lemon pepper cream crostini

**This makes an elegant alternative to the usual smoked salmon canapés. The cream has a punchy pepper kick to it with cool lemon undertones. Tossing the salmon in the dill gives it a lovely fresh appearance.**

Preheat the oven to 190°C (375°F) Gas 5. To make the crostini, brush both sides of each slice of bread with olive oil and spread out on a baking sheet. Bake for about 10 minutes until crisp and golden. Let cool, then keep in an airtight container until ready to use. It is best to reheat them in the oven before adding the topping.

To make the lemon pepper cream, pound or grind the peppercorns as finely as possible. Beat the mascarpone with the ground pepper, add the milk and lemon rind and beat again. Season with salt and lemon juice to taste. Chill until needed.

Toss the smoked salmon with the chopped dill. Spread the crostini with the lemon pepper cream and place a mound of smoked salmon on top. Squeeze over a little more lemon juice and serve immediately.

250 g thinly sliced smoked salmon

2 tablespoons chopped fresh dill

sea salt

**for the crostini:**

1 Italian sfilatino or thin French baguette, thinly sliced diagonally

extra virgin olive oil, for brushing

**for the lemon pepper cream:**

2 teaspoons black peppercorns

75 ml mascarpone cheese

75 ml milk

finely grated rind and juice of 1 lemon

**Serves 6**

This is the Italian equivalent of Mexican tacos but turned upside down. The crisply fried polenta bases remain soft in the middle and are topped with chunky guacamole and smokey pan-grilled strips of chicken. The contrast of flavours and textures is amazing.

# pan-grilled chicken and guacamole
## on crisp polenta crostini

350 g skinless, boneless chicken breasts

2 tablespoons lemon juice

1 garlic clove, crushed

2 tablespoons olive oil

1 quantity Polenta Crostini (see page 9)

butter, for frying, or olive oil or melted butter, for brushing

### for the guacamole:

2 ripe avocados

6 spring onions, chopped

1 medium tomato, skinned, seeded and chopped

2 tablespoons chopped fresh coriander

lemon juice

sea salt and freshly ground black pepper

### to serve:

3 cherry tomatoes, halved

coriander leaves

**Serves 6**

Cut the chicken into finger-thin strips and mix with the lemon juice, garlic and olive oil. Leave to marinate while you make the guacamole.

Halve the avocados, remove the stones and peel off the skin. Place the flesh in a bowl and mash to a rough texture with a fork. Mix in the spring onions, chopped tomato and coriander. Season to taste with lemon juice, salt and pepper. Don't make this too far in advance as it discolours quickly.

To cook the polenta crostini, melt a little butter in a hot, non-stick frying pan and cook until crisp, turning once. Alternatively, brush both sides with olive oil or melted butter and pan-grill, turning once, for a char-grilled taste.

To cook the chicken, heat a stove-top grill pan until smoking. Add the chicken strips and pan-grill on one side only for 2–3 minutes, without moving, until cooked.

Spread the crostini with some guacamole then top with chicken strips. Top each one with half a cherry tomato and some coriander leaves. Serve immediately.

**meat and poultry**

# grilled fig and prosciutto
## bruschetta **with rocket**

This combination of caramelized figs and crisply barbecued prosciutto is irresistible. The figs are best cooked on a barbecue, but you can use a stove-top grill pan or a grill – just get the right amount of charring on the figs.

To make the bruschetta, grill, toast or pan-grill the bread on both sides until lightly charred or toasted. Rub the top side of each slice with the cut garlic, then drizzle with olive oil. Keep them warm in a low oven.

Take the figs and stand them upright. Using a small, sharp knife, make two cuts across each fig not quite quartering it, but keeping it intact at the base. Ease the figs open and brush with balsamic vinegar and olive oil. Put the figs cut side down on a preheated barbecue or stove-top grill pan and cook for 3–4 minutes until hot and slightly charred – don't move them during cooking. Alternatively, place the figs cut side up under a really hot grill until browning and heated through.

While the figs are cooking, place half the slices of prosciutto on the barbecue or stove-top grill pan, or under the grill and cook until frazzled. Remove and keep warm while cooking the remaining slices. Place two figs, three pieces of prosciutto and some rocket on each slice of bruschetta. Cover with Parmesan shavings and drizzle with olive oil. Serve immediately.

4 thick slices country bread, preferably sourdough

2 garlic cloves, halved

extra virgin olive oil, for drizzling, plus extra for brushing

8 ripe fresh figs

2 tablespoons balsamic vinegar

12 slices prosciutto

100 g rocket

sea salt and freshly ground black pepper

shavings of Parmesan cheese, to serve

**Serves 4**

# chorizo with crunchy saffron potatoes
## on bruschetta

This pretty-coloured substantial snack has its origins in Spain. The secret ingredient is a mild smoked paprika called *pimentón*, which gives the potatoes an interesting depth of flavour. If you can't get hold of it, use sweet paprika instead.

Peel the potatoes and cut into 2.5 cm cubes. Cook in boiling salted water for 5–7 minutes until they are almost cooked but still slightly firm in the middle.

While the potatoes are cooking, make the bruschetta. Grill, toast or pan-grill the bread on both sides until lightly charred or toasted. Rub the top side of each slice with the cut garlic, then drizzle with olive oil. Keep them warm in a low oven.

Drain the potatoes well. Heat the sunflower oil in a large frying pan, add the potatoes and fry them over a medium heat for about 5 minutes, turning from time to time, until a light golden brown. Sprinkle over the saffron water and continue to cook for 3–4 minutes. Next, add the ground cumin and pimentón and cook for a further 5 minutes, tossing and turning the potatoes until they build up a nice spicy crust. Add the chorizo and cook for another 5 minutes until it is heated through.

Season well with salt and pepper, then spoon the mixture over the bruschetta. Scatter with fresh coriander and serve immediately.

350 g potatoes

4 thick slices country bread, preferably sourdough

2 garlic cloves, halved

extra virgin olive oil, for drizzling

2–3 tablespoons sunflower oil

large pinch saffron threads soaked in 3 tablespoons hot water for 15 minutes

1/2 teaspoon ground cumin

1/2 teaspoon pimentón (smoked paprika)

175 g chorizo, sliced or cubed

sea salt and freshly ground black pepper

chopped fresh coriander, to serve

**Serves 4**

These are delicious mouthfuls of melting mozzarella swathed in Parma ham. They taste good served cold with the addition of a thin slice of ripe melon on top, but heating them up transforms them.

# prosciutto-wrapped bocconcini crostini

Preheat the oven to 190°C (375°F) Gas 5. To make the crostini, brush both sides of each slice of bread with olive oil and spread out on a baking sheet. Bake for about 10 minutes until crisp and golden. Let cool, then keep in an airtight container until ready to use. It is best to reheat them in the oven before adding the topping.

Put a sage leaf on top of each bocconcini or mozzarella cube and season with salt and pepper. Cut each slice of ham into three equal pieces and wrap up a piece of cheese in each one.

Mix the mustard and balsamic vinegar together and spread on the crostini. Pop two mozzarella parcels on top of each crostini and put on a baking sheet. Bake in the oven for 3–5 minutes or until the cheese just melts. Serve immediately, topped with more sage leaves.

1 Italian sfilatino or thin French baguette, sliced into thin rounds

extra virgin olive oil, for brushing

24 fresh sage leaves, plus extra to serve

24 bocconcini cheeses or 3 regular mozzarella cheeses, cubed

8 slices prosciutto or Parma ham

3 tablespoons grain mustard

1 teaspoon balsamic vinegar

sea salt and freshly ground black pepper

**Serves 6**

To make the salsa verde, pound the salt and garlic with a mortar and pestle until creamy. Stir in the anchovies, parsley, mint, basil, capers, olive oil, lemon juice and pepper. Transfer to a jar and pour a layer of olive oil on top to exclude the air. This will keep for up to a week in the refrigerator.

To make the bruschetta, grill, toast or pan-grill the bread on both sides until lightly charred or toasted. Rub the top side of each slice with the cut garlic, then drizzle with olive oil. Keep them warm in a low oven.

Wrap the beef tightly in plastic kitchen wrap and put into the freezer for 20 minutes or until just beginning to freeze. Using a very sharp, thin-bladed knife, slice the beef into paper-thin slices (the part-freezing will make this easier). If you find this difficult, cut it as thinly as you can, then bat it out between two sheets of plastic kitchen wrap, without breaking through the flesh. This should be done at the last minute, or the meat will discolour.

Brush the bruschetta with a little salsa verde, then drape the sliced beef over the top. Spoon on some more salsa verde and top with a mound of wild rocket and a few Parmesan shavings. Season with salt and pepper and serve immediately.

4 thick slices of country bread, preferably sourdough

2 garlic cloves, halved

extra virgin olive oil, for drizzling

250 g best fillet of beef, perfectly trimmed

100 g wild rocket

sea salt and freshly ground black pepper

shavings of Parmesan cheese, to serve

for the salsa verde:

1 teaspoon sea salt

2 garlic cloves, finely chopped

4 anchovy fillets in oil, rinsed

3 tablespoons chopped fresh parsley

3 tablespoons chopped fresh mint

3 tablespoons chopped fresh basil

2 tablespoons salted capers, rinsed and chopped

150 ml cold-pressed extra virgin olive oil, plus extra for sealing

2 tablespoons lemon juice

freshly ground black pepper

**Serves 4**

# carpaccio of beef with salsa verde on bruschetta

This colourful dish relies on using the best beef fillet you can buy, thinly sliced and served with the classic Italian caper and herb sauce. Carpaccio of beef was created by the original owner of Harry's Bar in Venice. The colours of the dish reminded him of the paintings of the Venetian Renaissance artist, Carpaccio and the name stuck. This is a lighter dressing than the original version, which included mustard and egg yolks.

# italian sausage with radicchio and taleggio
## on crisp polenta crostoni

There is nothing more delicious on a cool autumnal evening than a golden polenta crostoni fried or grilled until crisp, topped with succulent Italian pork sausage, covered with melting Taleggio cheese and sweetly soft radicchio. You could be in front of a roaring fire in the Tuscan hills.

Preheat a frying pan, grill or stove-top grill pan. Cut the polenta into four thick slices, slightly smaller than the size of your hand (these are now crostoni). To cook the polenta crostoni, melt a little butter in a hot, non-stick frying pan and cook until crisp, turning once. Alternatively, brush both sides of the crostoni with olive oil or melted butter and grill or pan-grill on both sides.

Quarter the radicchio and remove the bitter white core. Put the leaves cut side up on a preheated stove-top grill pan. Brush with olive oil and season with salt and pepper. Add the sausages to the pan and pan-grill for about 10 minutes until the sausages are cooked and the radicchio has softened and is a little charred.

Meanwhile, remove the rind from the cheese and slice thickly. Slice the cooked sausages thickly, too. Put the cooked polenta slices on a lined grill pan and cover with the sausage slices. Top each crostoni with a couple of sage leaves then a piece of radicchio, then cover each one with a layer of sliced cheese. Place under a hot grill and grill until the cheese is melted and bubbling. Serve immediately.

1 quantity Polenta Crostini (see page 9)

butter, for frying, or olive oil or melted butter, for brushing

1 small radicchio

2 tablespoons olive oil, for brushing

4 fat Italian pork sausages (or any other high-meat content butcher's sausage)

100–150 g Taleggio or Fontina cheese (or other nutty quick-melting cheese)

8 fresh sage leaves

sea salt and freshly ground black pepper

**Serves 4**

# other Italian snacks

# parmesan crisps

You'll never make enough of these thin, crunchy savoury crisps – the secret is not to cook them for too long. They are sometimes made in a frying pan, but it is much easier to bake them in quantity in the oven. They keep well in an airtight container. I prefer to use Grana Padano for this – it is cheaper than Parmesan and works just as well.

Preheat the oven to 200°C (400°F) Gas 6. Line a baking sheet with non-stick baking parchment. Spoon small mounds of grated cheese onto the paper at regular intervals. Flatten with the back of the spoon. Sprinkle a few fennel seeds or some chopped red chilli on top, if you like.

Bake for 3-6 minutes until golden. Remove from the oven and leave for a couple of minutes to set. You can curl them over a wooden spoon handle or rolling pin at this stage to give a more interesting shape, if you like. Carefully lift them off the paper. Let cool completely on a baking rack. These crisps will keep for up to 4 days if stored in an airtight container.

125 g freshly grated Grana Padano or Parmesan cheese

a few fennel seeds (optional)

1 red chilli, deseeded and finely chopped (optional)

**Serves 4**

A wonderful explosion of the flavours of sage and anchovy through crisp batter. These must be served virtually straight out of the pan. I like to use a packet of Japanese tempura batter for this – it is so light and crisp.

# deep-fried sage leaves

Wash and dry the sage leaves. Mash the capers with the anchovy paste and spread onto the darker green sides of 12 of the leaves. Press another leaf on top of the filling to form a sandwich.

If you're not using Japanese tempura batter, then make your own. Lightly whisk the egg and the iced water together. Add the flour and whisk again, leaving the mixture a bit lumpy. Do not allow to stand.

Heat the oil in a deep pan or wok until a piece of stale bread turns golden in a few seconds when dropped in. Holding the leaves by the stem, dip them into the batter and lightly shake off the excess. Place into the hot oil, a few at a time, and fry until crisp and barely golden. This will only take a few seconds. Drain on kitchen paper and serve immediately.

24 large sage leaves

1 teaspoon salted capers, rinsed

1 tablespoon anchovy paste

vegetable oil, for deep-frying

for the batter:

1 egg

150 ml iced water

125 g plain flour

**Makes 12**

# grissini

These long, thin crisp breadsticks originate from Turin in northern Italy. Once you have made your own, you will never want the bought ones in packets again.

Preheat the oven to 200°C (400°F) Gas 6. Roll the dough out thinly on a well-floured surface to form a rectangle. Cut into 5 mm strips along the long side of the rectangle. Lightly roll these strips with your fingers and taper the ends. Put them on a baking sheet, spacing well apart.

Brush the dough lightly with water and sprinkle with the flavouring of your choice. Bake for 5-8 minutes until crisp and brown. Let cool completely. Twist salami or prosciutto around the sticks, to serve, if liked.

1 quantity Basic Pizza Dough (see below)

salami or prosciutto slices, to serve

**flavourings:**

sea salt

sesame seeds

poppy seeds

cracked black pepper

**Makes about 40**

# basic pizza dough

In a medium bowl, cream the fresh yeast with the sugar and whisk in 125 ml warm water. Leave for 10 minutes until frothy. For other yeasts, follow the manufacturer's instructions. Sift the flour into a large bowl and make a well in the centre. Pour in the yeast mixture, olive oil and salt. Mix together with a round-bladed knife, then use your hands to bring the dough together.

Tip out onto a floured surface, wash and dry your hands and knead for 10 minutes until smooth and elastic. The dough should be quite soft, but if too soft to handle, add more flour. Place in a clean oiled bowl, cover with a damp tea towel and leave to rise until doubled in size – about 1 hour. Knock back and use as required.

12 g fresh yeast, 7 g dried active baking yeast or 1 sachet easy-blend yeast

pinch sugar

175 g Italian 00 flour or strong plain flour, plus extra for dusting

1 tablespoon olive oil

½ teaspoon sea salt

**Makes 1 x 25–30.5 cm thin crust pizza base**

These are a great example of Sicilian street food – little fritters made out of ground chickpeas. So popular throughout the Mediterranean, every country has a form of snack made with these versatile legumes. The fritters are crisp on the outside and soft in the middle. To taste their best they must be served hot and sprinkled with lots of sea salt.

# sicilian chickpea and rosemary fritters (*panelle*)

Lightly oil a cold surface such as a marble slab or the back of a large baking sheet. Have a spatula at the ready! Sift the chickpea flour into a saucepan. Whisk in the water slowly, making sure there are no lumps. Stir in the rosemary, and salt and pepper to taste. Bring to the boil, beating all the time, until the mixture really thickens and leaves the side of the pan (like choux pastry). Don't worry if you get lumps at this stage, they will disappear when you fry the panelle.

Now you need to work really quickly. Tip the mixture onto the oiled surface and spread it out as thinly and evenly as you can – aim to make it about 3 mm thick. Let cool and set.

When set, cut into small triangles or squares. To prevent them drying out, place them between layers of plastic kitchen wrap until ready to cook. Heat some oil in a wok or deep-fat fryer. The oil is ready when a piece of mixture will sizzle instantly when dropped in. Deep-fry a few panelle at a time, turning when golden brown. Drain on kitchen paper and sprinkle with salt. Serve hot.

300 g chickpea flour*

750 ml water

1–2 tablespoons chopped fresh rosemary

vegetable oil, for deep-frying

sea salt and freshly ground black pepper

**Makes about 40**

* Chickpea flour is known as gram flour in Asian shops.

# mozzarella in carozza

A classic Italian restaurant favourite, but this more rustic version is so easy to make at home. The mozzarella melts inside the crisp bread coat, revealing a surprise of sun-dried tomatoes and anchovies inside.

Arrange the mozzarella slices over 4 of the slices of bread. Scatter the sun-dried tomatoes, anchovy fillets and oregano over the mozzarella. Season well with salt and pepper, then put the remaining bread slices on top. Press down well.

Pour the beaten eggs into a large dish and dip the sandwiches in the egg, turning once to coat both sides. Leave them to soak up the egg for 30 minutes.

Heat the oil in a deep frying pan until a crumb dropped in sizzles instantly. Fry each sandwich for 1–2 minutes on each side until crisp and golden brown. Drain on kitchen paper and serve piping hot.

2 mozzarella cheeses, thickly sliced

8 thin oval slices country bread

8 sun-dried tomatoes, soaked until soft and cut into strips

8 anchovy fillets in oil, drained

2 teaspoons dried oregano

3 eggs, beaten

vegetable oil, for shallow frying

sea salt and freshly ground black pepper

**Serves 4**

# index

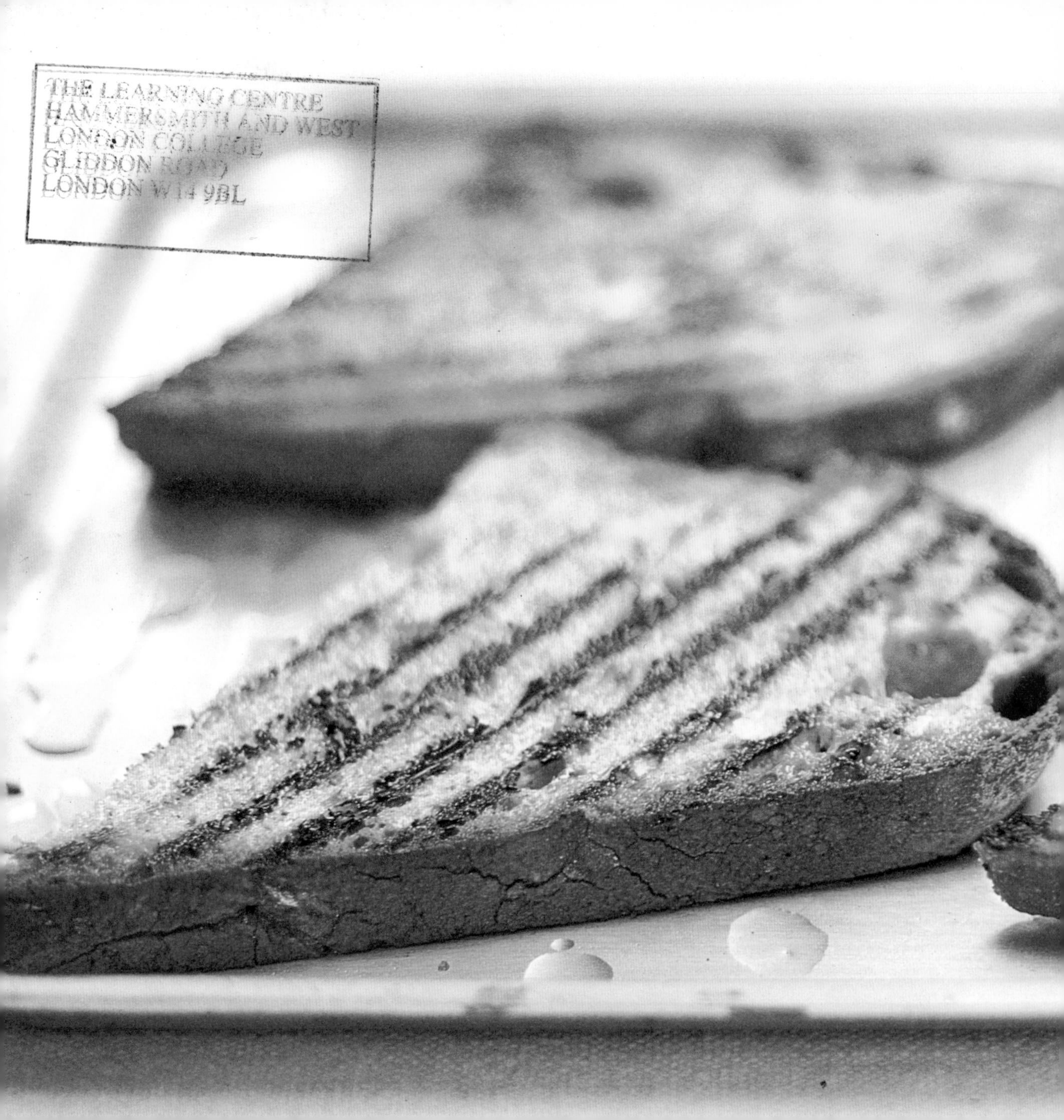